DISCOVER

Deserts

Contributing Writer
Jennifer Vogelgesang

Consultant
Howard E. Lawler

Publications International, Ltd.

Louis Weber, C.E.O.
Publications International, Ltd.
7373 N. Cicero Avenue
Lincolnwood, Illinois 60646

Manufactured in USA

8 7 6 5 4 3 2 1

ISBN 1-56173-424-1

Photo credits:

Front cover: **Comstock** (center & bottom); **E.R. Degginger/Animals Animals** (top).

Back cover: **Tom & Michele Grimm/International Stock Photography** (bottom); **D. Marklin/FPG International** (top).

Animals Animals: Anthony Bannister: 30 (bottom left); Dick Michael: 27 (center); K. Gillett: 31 (bottom); Rodger Jackman: 27 (bottom); Alan G. Nelson: 31 (top); Fred Whitehead: 18 (center); **Kent & Donna Dannen**: Front end sheets (right center), table of contents (top left), 10 (top & center), 12 (top & bottom), 17, 19 (left), 21 (top); **FPG International**: 21 (bottom left), 24 (top), 26 (bottom), 30 (top); Laurance B. Aluppy: 15 (bottom); Dave Bartruff: 4 (top); Jon Brenneis: 38 (bottom), back end sheets (top left); Bruce Byers: 19 (right); Tom Campbell: Back end sheets (center); Willard Clay: 11, 23 (top); Paul Degreve: 9 (center), 13 (bottom); Art Montes DeOca: Table of contents (bottom left), 39 (top & center), back end sheets (bottom left); Farrell Grehan: 43 (right); Richard Harrington: 37 (bottom); Randall Hoover: 32 (bottom); S. Kanno: 6 (top right); Lee Kuhn: 22 (bottom); Dick Luria: 36 (top); Neal & Mary Jane Mishler: Back end sheets (bottom right); E. Nagele: 10 (bottom); David·Noble: 6 (bottom), 25; O'Brien & Mayor Photography: Front end sheets (bottom left), 34 (top); Stan Osolinski: 13 (top), 18 (top), 19 (bottom), 32 (center); Martin Rogers: 37 (center); Barry Rosenthal: 8 (top); Leonard Lee Rue III: 9 (bottom), 22 (top), 33 (top right & bottom); M. Sutton: 36 (bottom); Ron Thomas: 14; Marv Wolf: 38 (top); Nikolay Zurek: 35; **International Stock Photography**: 38 (center); Dennis Fisher: 7 (bottom), 32 (top); Michele & Tom Grimm: 34 (bottom); D. Higgs: 27 (top); Kit Luce: 21 (bottom right); Donald L. Miller: 36 (center); Steve Myers: 30 (bottom right); Wilson North: 16 (top); Tom O'Brien: 39 (bottom); Len Rhodes: 37 (top); Roger Markham-Smith: 5; Michael Von Ruber: 15 (top); **Howard Lawler:** 4 (center), 9 (top right), 16 (center), 18 (bottom), 20, 23 (bottom left), 24 (center), 26 (top), 28 (top & center), 29 (top left); **Zig Leszczynski:** Front end sheets (top left & bottom right), 4 (bottom), 8 (bottom), 16 (bottom), 23 (bottom right), table of contents (top right & left center & right center), 24 (bottom), 28 (bottom), 29 (bottom left & bottom right), 31 (center), 33 (top left), 40 (bottom left), 42 (top); **Dan McCoy/Rainbow:** 6 (top left); **Robin White/FotoLex Associates:** Front end sheets (top right), Table of contents (bottom right), 7 (top), 40 (top & bottom right), 41, 42 (bottom left & bottom right), 43 (left), back end sheets (top right).

Illustrations: Pablo Montes O'Neill

Jennifer Vogelgesang holds a Bachelor of Science degree in wildlife ecology and agricultural journalism from the University of Wisconsin-Madison. She writes for *Ducks Unlimited* magazine and is editor and contributing writer for *Puddler,* a wetland wildlife magazine for children.

Consultant Howard E. Lawler is the Curator of Herpetology, Ichthyology, and Invertebrates for the Arizona-Sonora Desert Museum in Tucson, Arizona, and holds a Bachelor of Science degree from Belmont College, Nashville, Tennessee. He is a member of the Desert Tortoise Council and Desert Fishes Council and consulted the National Geographic Society's *Creatures of the Desert World.*

CONTENTS

WHAT IS A DESERT? • 4

Deserts of the World • Desert Weather • The Living Desert

DESERT LANDSCAPES • 10

Desert Plants • Desert Waters • Desert Formations • Desert Winds

IN THE DAYTIME • 16

Daytime & Nighttime Animals • Early Morning • Midday • Late Afternoon

AT NIGHT • 24

Insects & Arachnids • Bats • Reptiles • Mammals • Desert Dogs • Desert Cats

THE DESERT'S RICHES • 34

Metals • Minerals • Oil • Other Sources of Energy

LAND UNDER PRESSURE • 40

Artificial Deserts • Endangered Natural Deserts

GLOSSARY • 44

WHAT IS A DESERT?

Many people think of deserts as dry, hot places covered with sand. They think deserts are flat, empty lands where few things live. Do you think of deserts this way? If so, a look at some of the world's deserts would surprise you. There is more to many deserts than sun, sand, and silence.

In fact, deserts are far from empty. They are home to a surprising number of plants, animals, even people. Many of the plants and animals found in deserts are found nowhere else in the world.

Deserts cover about one-seventh of the earth's surface. Every continent except Europe has one or more desert regions. The largest desert, called the Sahara (suh-HAR-uh), is nearly as big as the United States!

4

DESERTS OF THE WORLD

The Australian desert is a harsh place. Few plants grow here because the weather is so dry and hot.

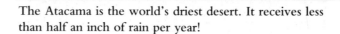

The Atacama is the world's driest desert. It receives less than half an inch of rain per year!

The Mohave is one of the North American deserts. Many of its plants, like this yucca, grow nowhere else in the world.

The world has 12 main desert regions. Three of them are found in Africa. The Sahara stretches across northern Africa, and the Namib (nah-MEEB) and Kalahari (KAHL-uh-HAH-ree) deserts are in southwest Africa.

A fourth major desert covers the center of Australia. The Australian Desert is the world's second largest desert. In fact, most of Australia's lands are *semiarid*. Semiarid lands receive a little more rainfall than a desert.

Five major deserts are scattered across Asia. They are: the Arabian, the Iranian, the Thar (tahr) (in India and Pakistan), the Gobi (in China and Mongolia), and the Turkistan (TUR-kuh-stan) (in central Asia).

South America contains two major deserts. The Patagonian (PAT-uh-GO-nee-uhn) Desert is found in Argentina. The Atacama (AHT-uh-KAH-muh) Desert—the smallest of the 12 deserts—covers parts of Chile and Peru.

One major desert region is found in North America. It is actually made up of four deserts. The region covers the southwestern United States and northwestern Mexico. The four deserts are called the Great Basin Desert, the Mohave (mo-HAHV-ee) Desert, the Sonoran (suh-NOR-uhn) Desert, and the Chihuahuan (chuh-WAH-wuhn) Desert.

Some deserts look very "typical." They have vast stretches of sand and waves of dunes. Much of the Arabian Desert looks like this. So do parts of the Sahara. Some areas of the North American deserts are covered with sand and dunes. Desert sands are many colors, from gray to tan, gold, and rose.

Most of the world's deserts are rocky, not sandy. Like sand, desert rocks come in many beautiful colors. They also come in many sizes and shapes, from gravel to snow-capped mountains. Caves, canyons, and strange, twisted rock formations add special beauty to deserts.

Desert landscapes change with the seasons. In some deserts, such as the Mohave, summers are hot and dry. Winters bring milder temperatures and, hopefully, rain. In other deserts, rains visit in summer. Those deserts come to life in early fall. Some, like the Sonoran Desert, have two rainy seasons, one in winter and the other in late summer.

Plants and animals have only a few weeks after rain falls to produce seeds or young before the desert dries again. Deserts look anything but empty during this time. Carpets of flowers add brightness to the desert's earthy tones. Animals come out of hiding.

Sandy deserts look harsh and exotic. It is no surprise most movies and books show deserts this way.

The desert landscape blooms with life after a spring rain.

The world's deserts have many faces. Some are covered with shifting dunes. Others are rocky and have more plants.

7

DESERT WEATHER

Deserts often go years without rain. In fact, some desert areas have gone 25 years or more without a single drop of it!

Odd as it seems, the frozen lands far to the north and south qualify as deserts. Most of the water there is locked up as snow and ice. So, these polar lands are very "dry." Polar "deserts" are called *tundra* (TUHN-druh).

All deserts have one thing in common no matter where they are. Deserts are *arid* (AR-uhd), which means they are very dry. Less than 10 inches of rain fall across desert regions each year.

Most deserts are very hot. Daytime air temperatures of 100 degrees Fahrenheit or more are common. The ground itself becomes 30 to 50 degrees hotter than the air! Why do deserts get so hot? Deserts lack many things that normally block the sun's heat. For example, moisture in the air "soaks up" some of the sun's heat. So do bodies of water such as lakes. Desert air and desert surfaces are very dry.

Clouds also block the sun's heat. But few clouds float above most deserts. There is rarely enough moisture in the air above the desert for clouds to form.

Deserts may become quite cold at night. The ground loses its heat once the sun goes down. Without moisture, clouds, or plants to trap the heat at the surface, it escapes. Temperatures can drop 50 degrees in deserts at night.

Some deserts are cooler than the others. They are usually located at higher altitudes or farther from the equator than hot deserts. The Gobi (GO-bee) Desert in central Asia is a high-altitude desert.

THE LIVING DESERT

Deserts are certainly harsh places to live. The heat is dangerous, and water is scarce. Even so, an amazing number of plants, animals, and even people, call the desert home.

 Each of the world's desert regions contains a unique mixture of living things. Many desert species of plants and animals exist only in arid lands.

All desert creatures have special ways of surviving heat and *drought* (drowt). Most have bodies designed to live on very little water. They also have tricks for finding and saving water and for avoiding heat.

The camel is well known for its ability to live on very little water. Camels can go days or even months without drinking water. The plants they eat contain all the liquid they need. Camels hardly sweat, so they lose little moisture.

Deserts seem forbidding to people who live in more "comfortable" parts of the world. But many plants and animals survive and even thrive in the desert. The special ways these creatures mold themselves to desert life make the earth's arid lands unique.

Cactus plants grow only in deserts—and only in North American deserts.

A camel's hump is filled with fat, not water, as many people believe.

Some of the driest desert regions lack any sign of life. But most deserts support more life than you might think.

Coyotes have many tricks for surviving in the harsh desert lands. They sleep during the daytime to avoid the desert's heat.

DESERT LANDSCAPES

form over time. Today's deserts were not always arid lands. Before changes in the earth's climate caused these regions to dry out, they looked much different. Some were actually covered by water. Others were grasslands, forests, or jungles. The animals that roamed these regions millions of years ago were unlike those found there now.

It has taken many thousands of years for deserts to develop their barren look. The desert landscape changes very slowly. But it does change and is still changing today.

Temperature, wind, and water shape desert lands. These forces crack, cut, and carry away pieces of the desert surface. Unique land features form this way.

10

DESERT PLANTS

Some desert landscapes lack any sign of plants. These dry lands are simply too harsh to support life.

All desert plants have tricks for dealing with great heat and long periods of dryness, or drought. Many small desert plants appear on the landscape only when heavy rains fall. These plants, which include grasses, shrubs, and flowering plants, "wait out" periods of drought underground. They exist for months or even years as seeds buried in the soil. When rains come, these seeds spring to life.

They quickly grow into adult plants and shed a new batch of seeds. Then they die. All this happens within a few weeks.

Other plants remain above ground to battle the desert's dryness head-on. These drought-fighting plants include trees, shrubs, and cacti (KAK-ty). The cacti are the best-known desert plants. Cacti are able to store large amounts of water after a rainfall. They can survive months or even years without running out of water.

The biggest cacti are the cardón (kar-DON) and the saguaro (suh-WAHR-oh). Both are found only in the Sonoran Desert. They can weigh as much as ten tons! And most of this weight is water! Saguaros grow extra roots to suck up rain shortly after it falls.

The saguaro can grow up to 50 feet in height.

DESERT WATERS

The desert has few permanent bodies of water. Rivers and streams do run through some desert regions. But most rivers and streams dry up as they cross the desert.

A few permanent lakes can also be found in arid lands. The Great Salt Lake in Utah and the Dead Sea near Israel are two examples.

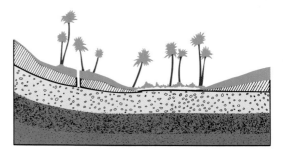

There is actually a lot of water trapped in layers of rock under the desert surface. Water collects in spongelike rocks that are filled with tiny holes and cracks. These rocks are called *aquifers* (AK-wuh-furz).

When rain falls in the desert, some of it sinks down, or seeps, into aquifers. Today's aquifers may hold water that fell as rain thousands of years ago.

Wherever water from an aquifer reaches the desert surface, an *oasis* (o-AY-suhs) forms. The land around an oasis doesn't look very much like a desert. It is green with plant life. And it is busy with the activities of animals and people. An oasis may be large, or it may be little more than a damp spot of sand. Some oases support entire civilizations.

A desert rainstorm can be a beautiful sight. The plants soak up as much water as they can while the storm lasts. They may not receive another rainfall for a full year.

Rainfall in deserts is unpredictable. Some deserts may go many years without it. A desert may get all its rain for the year from a single storm.

The oasis formed by the Nile River in Egypt has supported civilization for thousands of years.

13

DESERT FORMATIONS

The famous Grand Canyon in northwestern Arizona is the work of a rare, permanent desert river.

For millions of years, the Colorado River has cut its way into layer after layer of rock, gradually deepening and widening its channel. Now that channel is the Grand Canyon. It is more than a mile deep and almost 20 miles wide in some places!

After the storm, rainwater washes over the desert. It cuts, or *erodes*, channels in the soil and even in layers of soft rock. These channels are called *washes* or *arroyos* (uh-ROY-oz) in North America. Arroyos typically have steep walls and flat floors. Floods gush through these arroyos time and again, cutting deeper and deeper to form canyons.

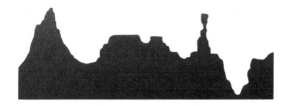

Desert mountain ranges often have many canyons, carved by the flow of rainwater. As the runoff (water that runs off the mountain) reaches the base of a mountain, it begins to slow down. At this point, the water leaves behind piles of boulders and large rocks it has carried. As the water spreads over the flat land, it dumps its load of sand and other fine bits of soil. The piles of rock and sand that collect at the ends of canyons near mountain bottoms are called *alluvial* (uh-LOO-vee-uhl) fans.

Mesas (MAY-suhz) are another special feature of deserts. Mesas are flat-topped mountains. The word "mesa" means "table" in Spanish. Mesas develop when a flat area of land is cut into sections over time by water erosion. Mesas are topped by layers of hard rock that don't easily erode.

14

DESERT WINDS

Deserts are windy places most of the time. Like water, wind is a powerful force in shaping desert surfaces. Blowing winds lift and carry small grains of dry sand and even smaller bits of dust from the ground.

A dune begins to form when moving sand bumps up against an object in its path. The sand forms a pile over the object. More sand blows up one side of the mound and drops off the other.

If the winds that carry the sand blow in more than one direction, star dunes form. They look like stars with many points. Star dunes tend to stay in one place, even up to hundreds of years. The other types of dunes constantly move across the desert like waves. A "sea" of sand is called an *erg* (urg).

Sometimes blowing sand forms spinning cones called *dust devils*. And sometimes strong winds cause sandstorms.

Whenever sand blows, it erodes the surfaces of objects in its path. Many of the rock shapes that dot the desert surface are created by wind erosion. A special combination of wind and water can even carve holes in rocks. The rock then forms a natural arch.

Some sand dunes form a crescent shape around an object that blocks their path. That is, they look a bit like a crescent moon. The wind blows more sand over the dune's outer edges than over its middle—this is how the shape forms. These dunes are called *barchans* (BAR-kuhnz).

If a desert area is covered mostly by sand, the wind blows the sand into rippled patterns and higher mounds called *dunes*.

The longest natural arch is called Landscape Arch. It is located in Utah. This arch is nearly 100 feet high and 300 feet long—about as long as a football field!

15

IN THE DAYTIME,

the desert can seem like a very empty place. The animals are there, but they are hiding from the sun's rays. Some hide under rocks or in caves. Others rest in nests built in cacti, trees, and shrubs. Still others move underground. Few stay out in the open.

This is because desert animals must time their activities to avoid the heat. Some animals are active during the morning and late afternoon, when the sun is not so hot. Others are active at night. Each desert animal has its own special way of surviving. But all desert animals have one thing in common: Their lives are ruled by the desert's heat and dryness.

DAYTIME & NIGHTTIME ANIMALS

In deserts as in all places, different animals are active at different times. Some animals come out at night. Others are active during the day.

Animals can be grouped by the time of day they are active. *Diurnal* (dy-URN-uhl) animals are active mainly during daytime. *Crepuscular* (kri-PUHS-kyuh-lur) animals are also active by daylight, but are most active at dawn and late afternoon, or dusk. *Nocturnal* (nahk-TURN-uhl) animals are active mainly during nighttime.

Most desert animals disappear during the heat of the day. They have moved out of the sun to rest in cooler, shadier spots. When the sun sets, the desert will cool. The air may also become a bit more moist, or humid. That's when many animals will come out of hiding to "start their day."

Some desert animals move underground during dry, hot periods. They go into a sleeplike state that is called *estivation* (ES-tuh-VAY-shuhn). When an animal estivates, its body becomes dormant. This means the body's functions slow down. Breathing becomes slower, and the heart beats slower. Energy is burned more slowly, too.

Some desert animals become dormant during winter to escape the cold. This is called *hibernation* (HY-bur-NAY-shuhn). It is very much like estivation. Many desert animals hibernate *and* estivate. Frogs, toads, ground squirrels, and tortoises hibernate and estivate to avoid the desert's hottest and coldest temperatures.

Because bats and snakes hibernate and estivate, they are active mostly in spring and fall.

EARLY MORNING

Desert mornings are filled with activity. In the first few hours of light, the desert is still cool. Dawn's arrival is loudly announced by singing birds. They have spent the night resting. Now, they are ready to start their day.

At dawn, birds also move across the ground. A North American bird called the Gambel's quail travels in groups called *coveys* (KUHV-eez).

The roadrunner also covers ground in the early hours. It is a large, striped bird with a long tail and strong legs. Roadrunners are speedy—they run as fast as 15 miles per hour!

The roadrunner and the quail do fly, but only when they have to. Some desert birds cannot fly. They must depend on their legs for escape. One flightless bird of the desert is the ostrich. Ostriches live in the Sahara Desert.

Some birds take to the sky in the morning hours. Eagles and hawks circle overhead. They are watching for rabbits, snakes, ground squirrels, birds, and other small animals.

Birds get most of their water from the food they eat. Seeds, fruit, stems, leaves, and animal flesh contain much moisture. Some birds get enough water from the food they eat. But many birds also need fresh water. So, they must spend their mornings in search of a drink.

You can easily see birds in the desert. They sing from atop shrubs, trees, and cacti.

The quail scratch at the ground, looking for seeds. They may also eat insects, berries, and leaves.

The ostrich is a well-known bird. It is the world's largest bird, standing nearly eight feet tall. Ostriches can run as fast as 40 miles per hour.

Roadrunners hunt insects, baby birds, gophers, mice, and snakes. They are even able to kill rattlesnakes.

19

You may have to look in the branches of a tree to find the Clark spiny lizard. This agile reptile is one of the daytime lizards.

The regal horned lizard blends in with the colors of the desert to make it hard for predators to find.

Early morning is also a busy time for many insects. Insects are not as easily seen as birds. But insects out-number birds and all other groups of desert animals. Insects that are active during the day include ants, cicadas, termites, wasps, beetles, grasshoppers, and butterflies.

All but a few lizards are active during daylight hours. Lizards are mainly insect-eaters.

Lizards have many enemies. Most lizards can escape when grabbed by the tail—their tails simply break off! New tails grow in later.

Other reptiles also come out in early morning. A few snakes may be on the move. However, most snakes are nocturnal—they wait until dark to come out.

The desert tortoise walks along slowly, feeding on plants. The desert tortoise hardly ever drinks. But it will drink water when it finds some. The tortoise stores water in large bladders inside its body. Desert tortoises grow very slowly. They can live over 60 years!

Lizards are well suited for desert life. Some lizards are able to plug up their nostrils. This keeps sand from blowing into them.

The collared lizard can actually rise on its hind legs and run quickly to escape danger.

Ground squirrels and rock squirrels scurry here and there in search of seeds, fruits, and other plant material. Both of these small, furry creatures are *rodents*.

Rodents are animals that have a special set of teeth for chewing, or gnawing. They are very common in all the world's deserts.

Larger mammals also live in deserts. Some of them are active during the morning hours. In North American deserts, herds of mule deer move carefully and quietly. Sometimes, they travel in small groups.

Desert bighorn sheep also travel in groups. They have beautiful, curling horns. Both deer and bighorn sheep are *herbivores* (HUR-buh-VORZ). This means they eat plants.

The camel is one of the most familiar desert animals. Camels are perfect for the desert. They can go a long time without drinking. They have long eyelashes to protect their eyes from blowing sand.

How do camels last without water? Camels eat plants, which contain water. They also have fat stored in their humps. They break this fat down for energy and for water. When camels do drink, they drink a lot—up to 20 gallons at one time!

Many of the animals you see in the early morning seem to disappear by midday. The heat of the afternoon sun is too much for them.

Desert bighorn sheep hide high in the mountains. They can easily run over rocks and across ledges.

There are two species of camels. Arabian camels have only one hump. Bactrian camels, which live in Asian deserts, have two humps.

MIDDAY

The golden eagle keeps cool by soaring high above the desert during the hottest part of the day. Even from a great height, the eagle's sharp eyes can spot its prey on the ground.

The gilded flicker makes its home in a hole it drills in a tree or cactus. In the hottest hours, it cools off in its shady nest.

Most desert birds find places to rest until the sun begins to go down. Birds make their homes in many places, even underground tunnels.

Even thorny plants like the cactus of North America's deserts make good homes for birds. They may build a nest by drilling a hole in the cactus.

An old nest hole often becomes a new home for another animal. The new owner may be another bird, such as the tiny elf owl. Mice, rats, lizards, insects, or even a bat might also use the hole.

Eagles, hawks, and vultures may still be seen overhead at midday. These birds can be active even during the scorching afternoon hours. They soar on rising winds high above the desert. The air up there is much cooler.

It's surprising, but temperatures change quite a bit just inches above or below the desert surface. Many desert animals have long legs. Ostriches, camels, and deer are long-legged animals. They walk along with their bodies high off the ground. This helps keep them cool.

Just inches below the desert surface, temperatures can be much cooler. That's why so many desert animals, like the kangaroo rat, make their homes underground. The air in these homes is also more moist.

LATE AFTERNOON

It is late afternoon in the desert. The sun has started to sink in the sky. The temperature is dropping. Long shadows stretch across the land. Desert life begins to stir once more.

Birds begin to sing again. The ants come out of their nests. Other insects leave their shady hiding places. Lizards are on the move again. Squirrels come above ground. The mule deer and the bighorn sheep search for a last bit of food and water. For all of these animals, the day is coming to an end.

The Gila (HEE-luh) monster is often active at this time of day. It is one of two poisonous lizards in North America.

The Gila monster is a very large lizard. It grows to over eighteen inches long. The Gila monster moves very slowly until it finds food, such as a young mouse. Then the lizard quickly moves to grab it. The Gila monster holds onto the animal with its teeth. Poison flows through grooves in the lizard's teeth.

The Gila monster hibernates in winter and estivates most of the summer. It lives off fat stored in its tail. The Gila monster's tail actually gets smaller as it uses up the stored fat. When the Gila monster builds up a new supply, its tail becomes larger again.

As late afternoon turns to dusk, the desert world changes. Animals of the daytime world seek places to rest and hide from predators.

As the evening approaches, snakes slither out of the rocks.

The Gila monster's bite is painful but not deadly to humans.

23

AT NIGHT,

the desert comes alive. One of the best times to see desert animals is at night. The desert cools off when the sun goes down. Nocturnal animals come out from caves, trees, or burrows.

The desert is filled with sound at this time. Animals buzz, squeak, hoot, rattle, " " and howl. Sweet smells might float on the night air. Some desert plants are blooming. Their flowers attract insects.

There's also plenty to see—if you have a flashlight! The flash of shining eyes. Shadowy shapes darting through the sky. The tracks of a snake that passed by not long ago.

Yes, the desert is a very busy place at night.

INSECTS & ARACHNIDS

When a tarantula catches a victim, it poisons its prey. A tarantula's bite isn't dangerous to humans. It's like a bad bee sting.

Unlike tarantulas, some species of scorpions can be dangerous to humans.

Nighttime insects include katydids, moths, beetles, and many others. The katydid makes a buzzing noise by rubbing its wings together. Males do the "singing" most of the time. And they sing only at night.

Desert moths have spent the day hanging under leaves and branches. Now, they make visits to flowering plants that bloom at night. The moths are drawn to the flowers by sweet smells and special colors.

Spiders and scorpions are *arachnids* (uh-RAK-nuhdz). They are closely related to insects. Some desert spiders come out in the evening. When the weather is very hot, the tarantula spider moves only at night. Tarantulas are the world's largest spiders. They are covered with hairs that help them "feel" their surroundings.

Many tarantulas live in underground homes, or burrows. They spend most of their time there. The burrows are cool and moist. Even when the tarantula comes out to hunt, it stays close to its home.

Scorpions are also active at night. Scorpions are found in deserts worldwide. The scorpion has a poisonous stinger at the end of its abdomen.

When the scorpion finds an insect, it grabs it in its claws, or pincers, and stings it. When a scorpion has babies, she carries them on her back as they grow.

BATS

Bats are mammals, though they seem like birds because they fly. Bats are the only mammals that can fly.

Several kinds of bats are found in deserts. Some kinds of bats are *solitary*. This means they live alone. Solitary bats spend the day hanging in trees, buildings, or even in cactus holes. When they rest, bats hang head down.

Some kinds of bats are *colonial*. This means they live in groups. Some colonies can include thousands of bats. Bats may migrate out of the desert in winter. Or, they may hibernate.

Bats catch flying insects right in the air. They do not depend on their eyes to spot prey in the dark.

Bats locate insects using sound. This is called *echolocation*. The bat squeaks, creating a sound wave. The sound wave bounces off anything in its path. The sound returns to the bat, like an echo. It lets the bat know something is up ahead.

Colonial bats sleep in caves or old mine tunnels.

At night, bats swarm out of their resting places to feed. Thousands of bats leave their cave in search of insects to eat.

27

REPTILES

Most lizards are active during the daytime. Only the gecko, and sometimes the Gila monster, can be seen in the desert at night.

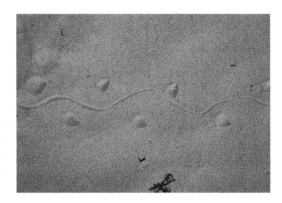

If you explore the desert at night, you might come across tracks left by the daytime animals. These tracks were left by a fringe-toed lizard.

Gila monsters are described as having "leaky" skin. They lose moisture through their skin more easily than other desert lizards. This is why they estivate and become nocturnal during the driest seasons.

Most lizards rest at night, but geckos do not. Geckos are found in many of the world's deserts. They get their name from the squeaky, chirping noise they make. Geckos are the only group of lizards that have vocal chords. Many other lizards hiss, wheeze, or whistle by exhaling air.

Most geckos can walk just about anywhere. They can move up and down smooth walls, and even across ceilings! They have special feet to help them. A gecko's toes are covered by brushy pads. Each pad is covered by tiny hairlike bristles with sticky ends. A gecko's feet also have claws for climbing in rough places.

Many people think the Gila monster is also a nocturnal lizard. As we have seen, this is not always true. The Gila monster is active mostly during the daytime, in the early morning and late afternoon.

So why do people think the Gila monster is nocturnal? Like many desert animals, the Gila monster sometimes changes its habits. At certain times of the year, you can see this lizard roaming the desert at night. When the weather is too hot and dry, the Gila monster cannot stand to be out during the daytime. The hot sunlight would cause it to lose too much moisture and die. So it comes out at night instead. At night, there is more moisture in the air.

Most snakes come out in the evening to hunt. Some of them are very poisonous. Coral snakes are dangerous. They have rings of black, red, and yellow. One type of coral snake lives in the North American deserts. Many snakes copy the coral snake's colors so other animals will avoid them.

Rattlesnakes are often nocturnal. They are dangerous desert dwellers. The rattlesnake sends poison, or venom, through the two long hollow teeth in its upper jaw. These teeth are called fangs. The poison forms in glands behind each eye.

In winter, rattlesnakes sometimes hibernate in large groups in underground burrows. Freezing temperatures are dangerous for them because they are cold-blooded reptiles.

There is a way to tell a real coral snake from a "fake" one. Left: A coral snake's bands go all the way around its body. Right: Most harmless snakes have bands just on their backs.

The rattlesnake's tail ends in a rattle. The rattle makes a buzzing sound when the tail shakes rapidly. A rattlesnake rattles its tail when it is alarmed and ready to strike.

The Western diamondback rattlesnake is one of the world's most dangerous snakes. It is to blame for more serious bites and deaths than any other snake in North America. It grows over six feet long!

The sidewinder is a rattlesnake that moves in a very special way. It lives in sandy desert areas. The sand makes it hard for the snake to slither. So, the sidewinder moves by making its body into a loop and "throwing" it sideways.

29

MAMMALS

The badger has strong front legs and claws. These make it a good digger. Badgers dig after rodents trying to escape underground.

The jackrabbit has very big ears. Heat escapes through the ears, helping the jackrabbit keep cool. Many desert mammals have big ears.

This is a rare glimpse of a golden mole above the ground. It spends most of its life tunneling under the desert's surface.

Jackrabbits' ears can turn left and right to pick up sounds. Their eyes are sharp, too. Jackrabbits eat cacti, grass, and low-hanging leaves.

The badger is also nocturnal. The badger has a territory it defends from other badgers. The territory is filled with holes. Each hole is a den. In the day, it rests in its den. The badger rarely rests in the same den two days in a row.

The Grants golden mole is a rodent that also has a special way of moving through the sand. The mole lives in the Namib Desert in Africa. It spends its whole life under the sand.

The golden mole hunts at night. The mole "swims" through the sand in search of insects and lizards to eat. It doesn't use its eyes and ears. It doesn't need them. How does the golden mole "see" its prey? It feels vibrations made by nearby animals moving over the sand.

Jackrabbits are also on the move at night. The jackrabbit is actually a hare, not a rabbit, although the two are very much alike.

How are rabbits and hares different? Rabbits are blind and have no fur when they are born. Hares can see and have fur when they are born.

The jackrabbit has long hind legs. These long legs help it run from danger with big leaps. A jackrabbit can reach speeds of 30 to 40 miles an hour.

Just as the jackrabbit is not a rabbit, the ringtail cat is not a cat. Ringtail cats are actually related to raccoons. Ringtails have rings of dark hair on their tails just as raccoons do.

Ringtail cats live in the North American deserts. They have very large eyes to help them see in the darkness. Ringtails eat rodents, birds, reptiles, insects, and plants.

Sometimes ringtails travel in pairs. They make dens in caves, in cracks along cliffs, in hollow trees, under rocks, or in empty buildings. The ringtail's nest is made of bark, grass, leaves, or moss.

The coati (kuh-WAHT-ee) also lives in North American deserts. It is also closely related to raccoons. Its tail is long and has rings. Coatis use their tails to help them balance. They wrap their tails around tree branches when they are climbing down headfirst.

The fat-tailed mouse is not really a mouse. It is actually a tiny *marsupial* (mar-SOO-pee-uhl). A marsupial is a mammal that has a pouch for carrying its young. Kangaroos are well-known marsupials. Kangaroos live in Australian deserts. So do fat-tailed mice. Fat stored in the mouse's tail breaks down into food when it is needed.

Ringtails make their dens in caves, cracks along cliffs, in hollow trees, under rocks, or in empty buildings.

The coati has a long snout for rooting out grubs and plant roots.

Coatis are active at night. They often run in groups of up to a dozen. They are great climbers and leap easily among desert cliffs.

What do a fat-tailed mouse and a camel have in common? Both of them store fat in their bodies that can be turned into energy when they need it. The camel stores the fat in its hump. The fat-tailed mouse stores it in its tail.

31

DESERT DOGS

The coyote hunts by day or night, depending on the temperature. It moves through the desert in search of prey during the cooler parts of the day.

The jackal is another foxlike hunter that lives in African deserts. Jackals look and act very much like coyotes.

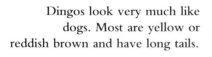

Dingos look very much like dogs. Most are yellow or reddish brown and have long tails.

North American deserts are home to the coyote, which looks like a dog. Coyotes spend hot days in a den underground. They eat whatever they can find—rodents, rabbits, snakes, grasshoppers, lizards, even grass. They can sometimes find water by digging holes in soft creeks and waterbeds. But most of their water comes from the food they eat.

The kit fox is a neighbor to the coyote. The kit fox has large ears to keep it cool. Its den is a sheltered place in the rocks or in a shallow hole.

The kit fox has a close relative in the Sahara Desert. It is called the fennec (FEN-ik) fox. The fennec fox is the world's smallest fox. It's smaller than a house cat.

The fennec fox has very large ears, like the kit fox does. In fact, a fennec fox's ears are bigger than its face! The ears are very good at hearing small rodents on the move.

Australian deserts are home to dingos. Dingos are wild dogs that were brought to Australia by its first people. Dingos hunt as family groups at night. They don't bark, but they do howl. They eat small kangaroos and rabbits.

DESERT CATS

Hunting cats also move across the desert at night. The bobcat is on the prowl. It has a short tail and long legs. Its pointed ears have tufts of hair at the tips.

The bobcat is a good climber. It will spend the night looking for rabbits, birds, mice, rats, and squirrels. Then, it will sleep through the day in a cave, under rocks, or maybe in a hollow tree.

The largest hunter in North American deserts is the mountain lion. These big cats are also called pumas or cougars. The mountain lion hunts deer, bighorn sheep, and smaller mammals. The lion's cry sounds like a human scream.

Mountain lions are uncommon in the deserts of the United States. People have hunted them and forced them to leave their old homes. Now they live mainly in protected areas and in mountains and forest regions outside of the desert. Mountain lions are more common in the Mexican deserts.

Although the mountain lion is strong and fierce, it usually stays away from people. For this reason, it is not thought to be dangerous to humans.

Cats are the largest hunters in the North American deserts. At night, they wander through the desert in search of prey.

33

THE DESERT'S RICHES

are there for those who know how to look for them. Deserts have a surprising number of things people need. And some of these things can't be found anywhere else. Even desert sand and rock is valuable.

Deserts have buried treasure! Diamonds, silver, gold, and copper are found there. So are many other things used to make everyday products. For example, oil from deep beneath the desert's surface helps us make thousands of products. Oil gives us power to drive cars. And it's turned into energy to light our homes.

The desert supplies other sources of energy. People turn energy from sun, wind, and underground heat into energy we can use.

Deserts are valuable, but fragile. Human activities must be limited to keep the desert's balance of life.

METALS

Today, silver, gold, and copper are still mined from desert regions worldwide. Surely, people will always admire the beauty of these valuable metals.

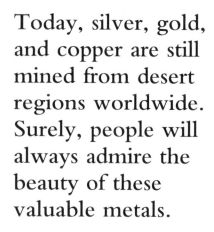

Like iron, copper is found in rocks called ore. Miners look for copper ore in the desert. Once it is separated from the ore, copper is one of the desert's treasures.

Most of the time, iron mines are deep pits in the earth. Sometimes, people build tunnels underground to look for iron.

Thousands of years ago, people began to search deserts for silver, gold, and copper. The people used these metals to make jewelry, tools, and weapons.

Silver and gold are mined from deserts in South Africa and in North and South America. Desert regions in the Soviet Union also contain gold. The Atacama Desert in South America has silver and copper.

Some of these deserts contain another metal called *iron*. Iron is one of the world's most useful metals. People build mines to find iron. Miners look for iron trapped inside rocks. Iron within rocks is called *iron ore*. The rocks are crushed to powder to separate the iron from the rock.

Uranium is another metal found in deserts. The United States and South Africa have large amounts of it. Uranium is used to make a special form of energy called *nuclear energy*. It is also used for making some kinds of weapons and for medical studies.

The world's largest supply of *bauxite* lies beneath the Australian Desert. Bauxite is used to make a light metal called aluminum. Giant shovels and bulldozers remove the earth that covers bauxite. Then, the bauxite is blasted loose with dynamite. It's loaded up, washed and dried, then shipped to factories.

MINERALS

Minerals are *inorganic*. This means they don't contain anything that was once alive. That is, they have no material from plants and animals.

The United States collects sand from its deserts. Chemicals, glass, paper, and concrete are made from sand. The United States also collects gravel and salt from its deserts.

Gypsum and soda ash are other minerals found at or near the desert surface. Gypsum is used to make plaster for walls and other building materials. Soda ash contains a form

of salt called sodium. Soda ash is used to make glass, soap, paper, and cleaning materials.

The Atacama Desert is rich in minerals called *nitrates*. Nitrates were once important in making fertilizers. Now, other materials are often used in place of nitrates for fertilizers. Nitrates have other uses. Camera film and some medicines and explosives contain nitrates.

Diamonds are one of the desert's rarest minerals. Only four areas in the world have good diamond supplies. The most important diamond supply is in the deserts of South Africa.

The Australian Desert also contains diamonds, as well as minerals called opals. Opals have many beautiful colors. They are used in jewelry.

The United States is the world's biggest salt producer. Salt is common in many desert regions. It coats the ground in layers of white chunks.

Diamond miners must dig through tons of earth to find one good diamond.

Many minerals are found in deserts. Examples of minerals include sand, salt, water, and stones.

37

OIL

Oil companies must drill holes to reach the oil and pump it to the surface.

Some of the oil in the United States is found in desert regions in California and Nevada. This oil derrick is in Utah.

Petroleum (puh–TRO–lee–YUHM) is the most useful thing that comes from deserts. Most people call petroleum by its common name, oil. Oil is found underground. It collects in the holes, or pores, of rocks buried deep in the earth.

Oil is used to make thousands of products. One product is fuel. Cars, airplanes, ships, and many other machines run on fuel made from oil.

These fuels also create heat and electricity for homes and businesses. Oil is also turned into other forms that go into things like carpets, plastics, and even toothpaste!

There are some problems with our use of oil for energy. First of all, the search for oil is expensive. Roads must be built so people can reach the places oil is found. Houses must be built for the workers. Food, water, machines, and tools must be shipped in. And once the oil is collected, it must be taken out of the desert.

More importantly, oil takes millions of years to form. Once it is turned into something else, it is changed forever. Someday, the world's oil supply will run out. Other sources of energy will have to take its place.

Oil refineries, like this one, are built in desert countries. This is where oil is transformed into fuel for cars and other machines.

OTHER SOURCES OF ENERGY

Deserts are sources of several kinds of energy. *Solar energy* comes from the sun. Heat and light from solar energy can be turned into electricity.

Rocks buried deep in the earth are very, very hot. Underground water flowing through these rocks turns into steam. The steam remains trapped under the earth's surface.

People drill beneath desert surfaces to reach steam trapped underground. They are also making their own steam by piping water down to the hot rocks. The steam is used to turn machines called *turbines* (TUR-buhnz). This makes electricity.

Energy from the earth's heat is called *geothermal energy* (JEE-o-THUR-muhl EN-ur-jee). People are working hard to make geothermal energy easy to use.

Desert winds are also used for energy. The wind turns windmills. The windmills turn turbines that pump water or make electricity.

Solar energy, geothermal energy, and wind energy make good replacements for oil. Their supplies will not run out, as oil is expected to. And, unlike oil, these forms of energy cause little or no pollution.

Some deserts also contain natural gas. Natural gas pollutes less than oil. But its supplies are limited, too. In the future, people will have to learn to rely less on energy from oil and natural gas. They will have to use more energy from sources that never run out, like the sun, the wind, and the earth's heat.

Deserts are great places to collect solar energy. The sun shines there almost all the time.

Above: Solar energy collected from a 20-mile area of desert can supply about a million homes with electricity!
Right: The sun's energy is collected by solar panels like these. Then it will be transformed into electricity.

Thousands of windmills collect the energy of the desert wind. Like solar energy, wind energy will never run out.

Land under pressure

is a problem in many parts of the world. More people live in arid lands than ever before. Most of these people live in countries that have too many people and not enough good land.

Artificial deserts are spreading in many places. People are not able to use the lands for growing food and raising animals.

Natural deserts are also changing. Their special landscape is being destroyed. And their plants and animals are being harmed by human activities.

People are working hard to turn artificial deserts into land that can be farmed again. And they are making sure natural deserts get the protection they need.

40

ARTIFICIAL DESERTS

More than 850 million people live in the world's desert regions! That's four times as many people as there are living in the United States. It is too many people for these areas to support.

This area is protected land. Animals are not allowed to graze here. The land was once an artificial desert because animals had eaten all the plants. Now, plants can grow again.

Trees are being planted. They keep the soil in place. Some of them serve as food and fuel.

Once the plants have been eaten, the soil is unprotected. Nothing is left to hold it in place. Wind and water wash the top layer of soil away. Plants do not grow there.

As a rule, deserts take millions of years to form. They develop slowly as the climate and the earth's surface change.

People are changing this rule. Human activities are turning some lands into places that look like deserts. This can happen quickly—in less than a hundred years.

Sometimes, poor methods of growing food turn farmland into an artificial desert. Or the land may be cleared of trees and other plants. Too many cattle, sheep, or other animals can destroy land, too. Usually, a drought makes these problems worse.

Nowadays, people understand that changes have to be made to stop the spread of artificial deserts. Scientists are helping people who live in arid regions learn how best to use the land. People are learning better farming and herding methods. Large areas of land are being set aside. Animals are not allowed in. This way, no piece of land is grazed too much.

These are just a few of the ways people are working to bring green land back from emptiness. Chances are, it will take longer to repair the land than it did to damage it.

ENDANGERED NATURAL DESERTS

People's activities are changing natural deserts, too. Even people who just visit deserts for their beauty are hurting it. Trucks and motorcycles leave permanent tracks in the Sonoran and Mohave deserts. The tracks destroy the special landscape. Tourists also leave behind trash.

Rare items made by ancient people are taken from deserts.

Some plants and animals have become rare. They cannot adjust to people being around. Pollution from mining and other activities kills them or destroys their homes. Sometimes people hunt them, so their numbers drop.

In North America, the government has set aside desert areas. This protects them. People who are caught destroying landmarks get in trouble. They must pay a fine. So must people who are caught dumping garbage, killing or disturbing wildlife, or doing other illegal things.

Some people think deserts cannot be changed or hurt. This is not true. We now know deserts are fragile and can easily be destroyed. Their unique plants and animals can easily be harmed. People must remember this whenever they are in the desert.

Many desert plants and animals live nowhere else in the world. This is why it's important to preserve our natural deserts.

Vehicles leave behind tire tracks that destroy the desert's natural beauty. They also churn up the ground in their path. This kills young plants and digs up seeds before they can take root.

GLOSSARY

Aquifer (AK-wuh-fur): An underground layer of rock that has holes in which water collects. An aquifer can also be an underground layer of sand or gravel that contains water.

Arachnid (uh-RAK-nuhd): An animal with eight legs, closely related to insects. Spiders, scorpions, mites, and ticks are arachnids.

Arid (AR-uhd): Something that is very dry. Deserts are arid lands that receive less than 10 inches of rain in a year.

Arroyo (uh-ROY-o) or **wash**: A channel that is cut into the land by the eroding force of flowing water. Arroyos have steep walls and flat bottoms.

Burrow: An underground hole or tunnel that an animal digs for shelter. Some burrows have many connecting tunnels.

Canyon (KAN-yuhn): A deep valley with steep sides that is carved over time by flowing water.

Crepuscular (kri-PUHS-kyuh-lur): Describes living things that are active at dawn and dusk.

Den: A sheltered place an animal lives in. Examples of dens include holes dug in the ground or a protected space between rocks.

Diurnal (dy-URN-uhl): Describes living things that are active during daylight hours.

Drought (drowt): A long period that passes without rainfall.

Dune: A hill of sand formed by blowing winds.

Erosion (i-RO-zhuhn): A process by which soil is blown or carried away by wind or water.

Estivation (ES-tuh-VAY-shuhn): Going into a sleeplike state during times of heat and drought. Estivating animals burn energy slowly, so they don't need food and water.

Evaporate (i-VAP-uh-RAYT): To change from a liquid or a solid material into an invisible gas. Water evaporates into vapor, an invisible cloud of moisture that hangs in the air.

Herbivore (HUR-buh-VOR): An animal that eats only plants.

Hibernation (HY-bur-NAY-shuhn): Going into a sleeplike state during wintertime. Hibernating animals can survive long periods without food and water.

Mammal (MAM-uhl): Member of a group of animals that includes humans. All mammals have hair, and their bodies produce milk to feed their young.

Marsupial (mar-SOO-pee-uhl): A mammal, such as a kangaroo, that has a special pouch on the outside of its body. The pouch is used to carry young.

Mesa (MAY-suh): A tablelike desert landform that has a flat top and steep sides. Over time, wind and water form masses through erosion.

Nocturnal (nahk-TURN-uhl): Describes living things that are active during nighttime hours.

Oasis (o-AY-suhs): A place where there is always water in a desert. An oasis can be formed where an aquifer touches the desert surface or by a river.

Rodent (ROD-uhnt): A mammal that has special teeth for chewing. Rodents' teeth never stop growing.